MW00903701

ACT Science Aspire Test Prep Book

Young Scholars Circle

This is a full-length mock test ideal for students who will take the ACT Science Aspire Early High School . It attempts to simulate a full-length test of ACT Science Aspire EHS content, format and test language and contains the type of science passages and the types of question items that the students might see in the actual exam, including the constructed responses. This book might be helpful for diagnostic purposes to see an overview of one's skills, and figure out a plan for test preparation.

Introduction .

This book contains an ACT Science Aspire Full-Length Mock Test. You will see five Science passages with three types of passage: research summaries, rata representation and conflicting viewpoints (most difficult for middle school students). Question categories include:

1. Interpretation of Data (IOD): Locating & Understanding, Inferring & Translating and Extending & Reevaluating
2. Scientific Investigation (SIN): Locating & Comparing, Designing & Implementing, Extending & Improving
3. Evaluation of Models, Inferences and Experimental Results (EMI): Inferences & Results, Evaluating & Extending

There are 34 multiple-choice questions and 6 constructed responses questions in this mock test.

If you really want to increase your score, you might want to consider taking a prep class. We have diagnostic test that you can take online to give you an overview of your skills. See the link https://youngscholarscircle.com/product/quant-q-practice-tests-self-paced-tutoring/

In the Northern Virginia area, ACT Science Aspire is administered to all aspiring applicants of Thomas Jefferson High School for Science and Technology (TJHSST).

Visit this link for our TJ Diagnostic Test that your child can take online (Quant Q, Reading Aspire and Science Aspire):

https://youngscholarscircle.com/product/tj-diagnostic-test/

In addition, you can either take our private one on one tutoring or attend some of our comprehensive and intensive classes.

For one on one class, visit this link below:

https://youngscholarscircle.com/product/testprep-tutoring/

For ACT Science Aspire Intensive Classes, visit the link below:

https://youngscholarscircle.com/product/tj-science-intensive/

Contact us at questions@youngscholarscircle.com or (571) 426-4639 for inquiries.

ACT Science Aspire Mock Test Answer Sheets

Time Limit: 60 minutes

Tear the answer sheets and use them when answering the mock test.

YOUNG
SCHOLARS
CIRCLE

Multiple Choice Answer Sheet

	A	B	C	D	QUESTION TYPE		A	B	C	D	QUESTION TYPE
1	O	O	O	O	EMI	21	O	O	O	O	IOD
2	O	O	O	O	IOD	22	O	O	O	O	IOD
3	O	O	O	O	IOD	23	O	O	O	O	IOD
4	O	O	O	O	IOD	24	O	O	O	O	SIN
5	CR Score_____				IOD -2 points	25	O	O	O	O	IOD
6	O	O	O	O	IOD	26	O	O	O	O	IOD
7	O	O	O	O	SIN	27	O	O	O	O	IOD
8	O	O	O	O	IOD	28	O	O	O	O	EMI
9	O	O	O	O	SIN	29	O	O	O	O	SIN
10	CR Score_____				SIN – 2 points	30	O	O	O	O	EMI
11	O	O	O	O	SIN	31	O	O	O	O	SIN
12	O	O	O	O	SIN	32	CR Score_____				SIN – 2 points
13	CR Score_____				SIN – 2 points	33	O	O	O	O	SIN
14	O	O	O	O	SIN	34	O	O	O	O	IOD
15	O	O	O	O	SIN	35	CR Score_____				SIN – 2 points
16	O	O	O	O	SIN	36	O	O	O	O	IOD
17	O	O	O	O	SIN	37	O	O	O	O	IOD
18	O	O	O	O	IOD	38	O	O	O	O	IOD
19	O	O	O	O	EMI	39	O	O	O	O	EMI
20	O	O	O	O	IOD	40	CR Score_____				SIN

Question Types	Total Score	My Scores	My Notes Areas of Strengths & Needs
SIN	22		
IOD	19		
EMI	5		
TOTAL	46		

CONSTRUCTED RESPONSES ANSWER SHEETS

#5

_____
_____
_____
_____
_____
_____

#10

_____
_____
_____
_____
_____
_____

13

_____
_____
_____
_____
_____
_____

#32

_____

_____

_____

_____

_____

_____

#35

_____

_____

_____

_____

_____

_____

#40

_____

_____

_____

_____

_____

_____

_____

ACT Science Aspire Mock Test 1

Time Limit: 60 minutes

Reading passage and data for questions 1-6:

Enzymes play an important role in human digestion. The organs of the digestive system have enzymes that function specifically for their pH of that environment. A pH from 0-6 is acidic, a pH of 7 is neutral, and a pH of 8-14 is basic.

Part of the Digestive System	pH Range	Amount of Time for Digestion
Saliva	6.5-7.5	Up to 1 minute
Stomach	1.5-6.5	1-4 hours
Duodenum	7-8.5	30-60 minutes
Small Intestine	4-7	1-5 hours

Enzyme	Macromolecules Digested
Amylase	Carbohydrates
Lipase	Lipids (Fats)
Trypsin	Protein

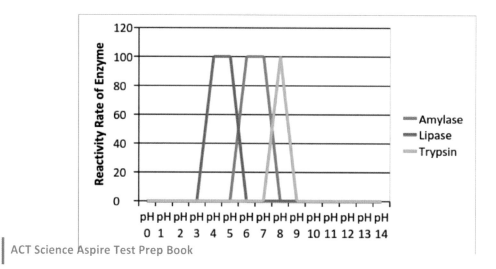

1. According to the data, which part of the digestive system does not provide a neutral pH environment for enzymes?
   a. Saliva
   b. Stomach
   c. Duodenum
   d. Small Intestine

2. Which enzyme is most effective in the duodenum?
   a. Amylase
   b. Lipase
   c. Trypsin
   d. None of the enzymes provided will be effective in the duodenum.

3. Papain is a digestive enzyme extracted from papaya that aids in the breakdown of proteins. Papain is most reactive at a pH of 6. Which part of the digestive system would papain be least effective?
   a. Saliva
   b. Stomach
   c. Duodenum
   d. Small Intestine

4. In what part of the digestive system are carbohydrates broken down?
   a. Saliva
   b. Stomach
   c. Duodenum
   d. Small Intestine

5. Explain which macromolecule takes the longest to digest and where the digestion occurs. Support your answer with details from the data.
   Constructed Response

6. What is the optimal pH for the digestion of carbohydrates?
   a. 4
   b. 6
   c. 7.5
   d. 8

Reading passage and data for questions 7-10:

A farmer is rotating his crops. Every year there will be a field that is not being used for crops grown for profit. The farmer wants to determine the best cover crop to plant in the unused field to prevent erosion. He divides the field into four plots and plants a different type of plant in each plot. The soil, amount of water, growing period, and amount of sunlight stay the same. The farmer measures the width of the plant bi-weekly until full grown to determine which plant provides the most cover and is best at preventing erosion.

Plant	Week 2	Week 4	Week 6	Week 8	Week 10
1	6	18	25	31	33
2	5	12	17	20	25
3	5	14	23	28	31
4	7	13	15	18	20

7. What is a possible hypothesis for this experiment?
   a. Plants grown for profit grow better than cover crops.
   b. Reducing wind prevents soil erosion.
   c. Wide plants reduce soil erosion.
   d. The amount of precipitation impacts soil erosion.

8. Based on the farmer's measurements, which plant would be best at preventing erosion?
   a. 1
   b. 2
   c. 3
   d. 4

9. What was the average increase in plant width every week?
   a. 1
   b. 2
   c. 3
   d. 6

10. Explain why a wider plant would decrease soil erosion. **Constructed Response**

11. If the farmer wanted to repeat his experiment next growing season, how could he modify experiment to validate his results?
   a. Measure the width of the plant and the length of the root system.
   b. Rotate the plants in the field.
   c. Use different plants.
   d. Increase the amount of water given to the plants.

Formulas and data for questions 12-19:

Density= Mass/Volume

Volume=Length x Width X Height

Density of Water= 1 gm/cm^3

	Mass in grams (g)	Volume in centimeters (cm)	Density in g/cm^3
Cube	420		
Rock	76		
Brick	1250		
Cylinder		32	
	Density g/mL		
Iron	7.8		
Aluminum	2.7		
Zinc	7.1		
Lead	11.3		

12. What is the density of the cube that is 4.2 cm x 4.2 cm?
   a. 74 g/cm^3
   b. 23.9 g/cm^3
   c. 100 g/cm^3
   d. 5.7 g/cm^3

13. Will the cube float in water? Explain your reasoning.
Constructed Response

14. Which physical property of a rock can be measured using a graduated cylinder? (see above)
   a. Mass
   b. Density

c. Volume

d. Hardness

15. What is the volume of the rock?
    a. 142 mL
    b. 152 mL
    c. 146 mL
    d. 156 mL

16. The balls in a beaker were determined to have a mass of 350g. The volume of the balls was 31 cm^3. What metal were the balls made of?
    a. Lead
    b. Zinc
    c. Iron
    d. Aluminum

17. If you are creating a raft that is 175 grams and you want it to float, what must the volume to have a density of 0.5 g/cm^3?
    a. 350 cm^3
    b. 87.5 cm^3
    c. .003 cm^3
    d. 174.5 cm^3

18. What is the mass of the cylinder if it is made of iron?
    a. 4.1 grams
    b. 249.6 grams
    c. 0.24 grams
    d. 361.6 grams

19. If you are filling a toy boat that has a mass of 25 grams and a volume of 600 cm^3 with marbles that each have a mass of 4 grams, how many marbles can you add to the boat before it sinks?
    a. 150
    b. 144
    c. 143
    d. 149

Reading passage and data for questions 20-25:

The Earth formed approximately 4.6 billion years ago. Initially, the atmosphere consisted of hydrogen, water vapor, methane and carbon oxides. The water vapor condensed 4 billion years ago to form oceans. About 1 billion years ago, blue-green algae in the ocean used the energy from the sun and carbon dioxide to undergo photosynthesis and released oxygen into the atmosphere. Some of this oxygen was split by UV radiation to form single oxygen atoms. These atoms combined with O_2 to form ozone. The ozone layer absorbs harmful UV rays and protects life on Earth from irradiation. The ozone layer was formed approximately 600 million years ago. Prior to this, life on Earth only existed in the ocean and the oxygen level in the atmosphere was 10%. The formation of the ozone layer enabled organisms to live on land.

Millions of Years Ago	Period
0-1.8	Quaternary
1.8-23	Neogene
23-66	Paleogene
66-145	Cretaceous
145-201	Jurassic
201-252	Triassic
252-299	Permian
Life on Earth	Period
1st Humans	Quaternary
Age of Mammals	Neogene
	Paleogene
1st Flowering Plants	Cretaceous
1st Birds	Jurassic
1st Mammals	Triassic
Abundant Reptiles	Permian

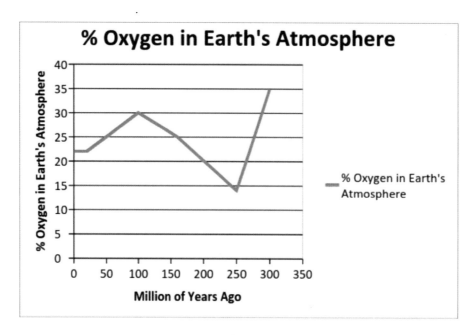

20. Which period had the highest levels of oxygen in the atmosphere?
    a. Quaternary
    b. Cretaceous
    c. Triassic
    d. Permian

21. During which period did the first warm-blooded animal appear?
    a. Triassic
    b. Quaternary
    c. Jurassic
    d. Permian

22. How many millions of years ago did the first flowering plant appear?
    a. 145-201
    b. 23-66
    c. 201-252
    d. 66-145

23. Make an inference using Table 1 and Table 2. How many millions of years ago did dinosaurs appear on Earth?
    a. 66-145
    b. 201-252

c. 252-299

    d. 145-201

24. What organism lived 650 million years ago?
    a. Flowering plants
    b. Blue-green algae
    c. Insects
    d. Reptiles

25. What was the percent of oxygen in the atmosphere when the first human appeared on Earth?
    a. 35
    b. 20
    c. 24
    d. 22

Reading passage and data for questions 26-33:

Apple scab is caused by the fungus, *Venturia inaequalis*. It produces dark brown lesions on the leaves, buds, and fruit of apple trees. Apple scab is a problem for apple farmers because it reduces fruit quality and yield. In the spring, the increase in moisture and temperatures causes the spores from the fungus to rise in the air and land on the tree surface. Secondary infections can also occur in the summer. In the winter, the fungus reproduces in the leaf litter creating a new generation of spores. Scientists are trying to determine the lowest dose of fungicide that can be used to reduce the reproduction rate of the fungus and the optimal temperature for the fungus reproduction. Over a 7 day period, at room temperature of 21°C, the fungus spreads 6 cm.

The scientists mixed various amounts of fungicide with agar and plated the fungus spores in petri dishes. They measured how far the fungus spread after 7 days.

Amount of Fungicide (mL)	Amount Fungus Spread (cm)
0.5 mL	6
1.0mL	5
1.5mL	3
2.0mL	3

The scientists performed a second experiment placing the petri dishes with fungus, without fungicide, in various temperatures for 7 days.

Temperature °C	Amount Fungus Spread (cm)
10	9 cm
15	10 cm
20	12 cm
25	12 cm

26. What is the minimum amount of fungicide that can be used to reduce the reproductive rate of the fungus by half?
    a. 0.5 mL
    b. 1.0 mL
    c. 1.5 mL
    d. 2.0 mL

27. What is the minimal optimal temperature for *Venturia inaequalis* reproduction?
    a. 10°C
    b. 15°C
    c. 20°C
    d. 25°C

28. What is a possible hypothesis for experiment #2?
    a. When *Venturia inaequalis* is plated in a petri dish with agar and fungicide, the highest level of fungicide will reduce the rate of reproduction.
    b. When *Venturia inaequalis* is plated in a petri dish with agar, the lowest level of fungicide at the highest temperature will increase the rate of reproduction.
    c. When *Venturia inaequalis* is plated in a petri dish with agar and fungicide, the highest level of fungicide at the highest temperature will increase the rate of reproduction.
    d. When *Venturia inaequalis* is plated in a petri dish with agar, the optimal temperature for the rate of reproduction is room temperature.

29. A 20 mL solution of agar + fungicide was used to fill each petri dish in the first experiment. What percent of the solution must be made up of minimum amount of

fungicide necessary to reduce the spread of the fungus by half?
    a. 7%
    b. 10%
    c. 12%
    d. 3%

30. The scientists are going to run a third experiment determining the optimal conditions to reduce the reproduction rate of *Venturia inaequalis* by half based on the first and second experiment, which of the following experiment should they run?
    a. An experiment growing *Venturia inaequalis* in petri dishes of agar containing 1.5mL of fungicide at various temperatures.
    b. An experiment growing *Venturia inaequalis* in petri dishes of agar containing various amounts of fungicide at various temperatures.
    c. An experiment growing *Venturia inaequalis* in petri dishes of agar containing various amounts of fungicide at 15°C.
    d. An experiment growing *Venturia inaequalis* in petri dishes of agar containing 2.0mL of fungicide at various temperatures.

31. What is the control in both experiments?
    a. The amount of fungicide used.
    b. The agar in the petri dish.
    c. The reproductive rate of the fungus without fungicide over 7 days.
    d. The reproductive rate of fungus at room temperature over 7 days.

32. The scientists would like to find out if the amount of light impacts the reproduction rate of *Venturia inaequalis*. Using the control from the first two experiments, describe a possible experiment that the scientist could perform.
    Constructed Response

33. Predict the amount of fungal spread if 2.5mL of fungicide are used.
    a. 8 cm
    b. 6 cm
    c. 5 cm
    d. 3 cm

Reading passage and data for questions 34-40:

Tennis balls used for tournament play must meet specific guidelines regarding size, weight, bounce and stiffness. A sporting goods company wants to design a faster tennis ball that will meet all of the requirements to be used for tournament play. Tennis balls are currently constructed of rubber with a hollow core, adhesive, and a nap. The nap consists of a mix of wool and artificial fibers. In the first experiment, scientists performed multiple trials and averages were determined using tennis balls with various nap consistency. The tennis balls were launched from a tennis ball machine with the same amount of force in ideal tennis conditions (18°C, 50% humidity and 5mph winds). The speed of the ball was measured in mph.

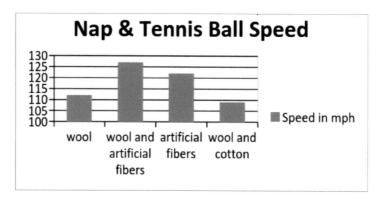

In the second experiment, scientists tested how humidity impacts the speed of tennis balls with nap made of the four different materials. They performed several trials on each nap at the four different humidity levels and determined the average in mph.

Table #1

Nap Material	20% Humidity	40% Humidity	60% Humidity	80% Humidity
Wool	125	112	108	102
Wool & Artificial Fibers	125	126	121	118
Artificial Fibers	120	122	121	122
Wool & Cotton	108	108	102	90

34. Based on the data, what type of nap produces the tennis ball that moves at the highest speed at 50% humidity?
    a. Wool
    b. Wool and artificial fibers
    c. Artificial fibers
    d. Wool and cotton

35. List four control variables in this experiment.
Constructed Response

36. Which nap is not impacted by humidity?
    a. Wool
    b. Wool & Artificial
    c. Artificial Fibers
    d. Wool Cotton

37. Which change in humidity resulted in the greatest decrease in speed for the wool & cotton nap?
    a. 20-40%
    b. 40-60%
    c. 60-80%
    d. The change is the same for all.

38. What type of nap material should not be used in tournaments that occur in humid conditions?
    a. Wool
    b. Wool & Artificial Fibers
    c. Artificial Fibers
    d. Wool and Cotton

39. The sporting goods company wants to create and sell tennis balls marketing them as the fastest tennis balls available based on the results of these two experiments. Based on the data, would this be an accurate statement?
    a. The statement is accurate because the scientists performed multiple trials and determined averages for each.
    b. The statement is not accurate because the scientists did not test the tennis ball nap materials at different temperatures and wind speeds.
    c. The statement is accurate because the scientists used controlled variables in the experiment.
    d. The statement is not accurate because the scientists did not use actual tennis players in the experiment.

40. Why did the scientists use a ball machine instead of tennis players to perform the experiment? **Constructed Response**

Answers and Explanations

Be sure to tally the type of questions that you missed on the front answer sheet and the correct total number of items. This will help you analyze your own strong and weak areas.

Reading passage and data for questions 1-6:

Enzymes play an important role in human digestion. The organs of the digestive system have enzymes that function specifically for their pH of that environment. A pH from 0-6 is acidic, a pH of 7 is neutral, and a pH of 8-14 is basic.

Part of the Digestive System	pH Range	Amount of Time for Digestion
Saliva	6.5-7.5	Up to 1 minute
Stomach	1.5-6.5	1-4 hours
Duodenum	7-8.5	30-60 minutes
Small Intestine	4-7	1-5 hours

Enzyme	Macromolecules Digested
Amylase	Carbohydrates
Lipase	Lipids (Fats)
Trypsin	Protein

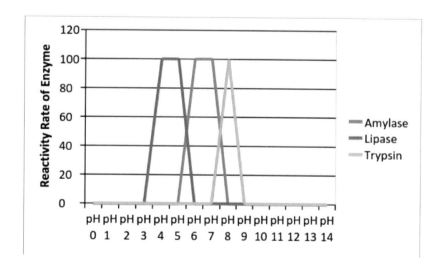

1   According to the data, which part of the digestive system does not provide a neutral pH environment for enzymes?
    a. Saliva
    b. Stomach
    c. Duodenum
    d. Small Intestine

Answer: B
pH of 7 is neutral and the stomach is acidic. (EMI)

2   Which enzyme is most effective in the duodenum?
    a. Amylase
    b. Lipase
    c. Trypsin
    d. None of the enzymes provided will be effective in the duodenum.

Answer: C
The duodenum has a pH of 7-8.5. Trypsin is most reactive at a pH of 8. (IOD)

3   Papain is a digestive enzyme extracted from papaya that aids in the breakdown of proteins. Papain is most reactive at a pH of 6. Which part of the digestive system would papain be least effective?
    a. Saliva
    b. Stomach
    c. Duodenum
    d. Small Intestine

Answer: C
The pH range of the duodenum is 7-8.5. Papain is most effective at a pH of 6. (IOD)

4   In what part of the digestive system are carbohydrates broken down?
    a. Saliva
    b. Stomach
    c. Duodenum
    d. Small Intestine

Answer: A
Amylase breaks down carbohydrates. Amylase is found in the saliva due to its optimal pH of 6.5-7.5. (IOD)

5   Explain which macromolecule takes the longest to digest and where the digestion occurs. Support your answer with details from the data.
    Constructed Response (IOD)

Scoring Guide

Score	Description
2	Lipase digests **lipids**. Lipase has an optimal reactivity pH of 4.5. The **stomach and small intestine** both have a pH range that would support the reactivity of the enzyme lipase.
1	Lipase digests **lipids**. OR explains that it occurs in the **stomach OR small intestine.**
0	Neither lipids nor stomach and small intestine are in the response.

6   What is the optimal pH for the digestion of carbohydrates?
     a.   4
     b.   6
     c.   7.5
     d.   8
     Answer: C

Carbohydrates are broken down in saliva, through amylase. The optimal pH is 6.5-7.5. (IOD)

Reading passage and data for questions 7-10:

A farmer is rotating his crops. Every year there will be a field that is not being used for crops grown for profit. The farmer wants to determine the best cover crop to plant in the unused field to prevent erosion. He divides the field into four plots and plants a different type of plant in each plot. The soil, amount of water, growing period, and amount of sunlight stay the same. The farmer measures the width of the plant bi-weekly until full grown to determine which plant provides the most cover and is best at preventing erosion.

Plant	Week 2	Week 4	Week 6	Week 8	Week 10
1	6	18	25	31	33
2	5	12	17	20	25
3	5	14	23	28	31
4	7	13	15	18	20

7   What is a possible hypothesis for this experiment?
     a.   Plants grown for profit grow better than cover crops.
     b.   Reducing wind prevents soil erosion.
     c.   Wide plants reduce soil erosion.
     d.   The amount of precipitation impacts soil erosion.

Answer: C

The farmer was trying to determine which type of cover crop would prevent soil erosion. (SIN)

8   Based on the farmer's measurements, which plant would be best at preventing erosion?
    a. 1
    b. 2
    c. 3
    d. 4

Answer: A

Plant 1 provides the most ground cover. (IOD)

9   What was the average increase in plant width every week?
    a. 1
    b. 2
    c. 3
    d. 6

Answer: C

The plant reached a width of 33 after 10 weeks, meaning the plant grew approximately 3 each week. (SIN)

10   Explain why a wider plant would decrease soil erosion.
Constructed Response (SIN)
Scoring Guide

Score	Description
2	The **wider plant covers more surface area** that protects the soil from wind erosion AND needs a **more expansive root system that holds onto the soil** and prevents erosion.
1	The wider plant covers more surface area OR the expansive root system holds onto the soil.
0	Neither the increase of surface area covered nor expansive root system are in the response.

11   If the farmer wanted to repeat his experiment next growing season, how could he modify experiment to validate his results?
    a. Measure the width of the plant and the length of the root system.
    b. Rotate the plants in the field.
    c. Use different plants.

d. Increase the amount of water given to the plants.

Answer: A

By measuring the width of the same plants in the same location and measuring the expanse of the root system, the farmer would have data on the amount of surface area covered by the plant and the expanse of the root system that holds on to the soil. (SIN)

Formulas and data for questions 12-19:

Density= Mass/Volume

Volume=Length x Width X Height

Density of Water= 1 gm/cm^3

	Mass in grams (g)	Volume in centimeters (cm)	Density in g/cm^3
Cube	420		
Rock	76		
Brick	1250		
Cylinder		32	
	Density g/mL		
Iron	7.8		
Aluminum	2.7		
Zinc	7.1		
Lead	11.3		

12 What is the density of the cube that is 4.2 cm x 4.2 cm?
   a. 74 g/cm^3
   b. 23.9 g/cm^3
   c. 100 g/cm^3
   d. 5.7 g/cm^3

   Answer: D
   Volume: 4.2 x 4.2 x 4.2= 74 cm^3 & Density: 420g/74 cm^3=5.7 g/cm^3 (SIN)

13 Will the cube float in water? Explain your reasoning.
   Constructed Response (SIN)
   Scoring Guide

Score	Description
2	**The cube will not float in water because the density of the cube is greater than the density of the water.**

1	**The cube will not float in water.** No explanation given.
0	The cube will float in water.

14   Which physical property of a rock can be measured using a graduated cylinder?

      a.   Mass

      b.   Density

      c.   Volume

      d.   Hardness

Answer: C

Liquid displacement using a graduated cylinder measures the volume of an irregularly shaped object. (SIN)

15   What is the volume of the rock?

      a.   142 mL

      b.   152 mL

      c.   146 mL

      d.   146 mL

Answer: C

The bottom of the meniscus reads 146 mL. (SIN)

16   The balls in a beaker were determined to have a mass of 350g. The volume of the balls was 31 cm^3. What metal were the balls made of?

      a.   Lead

      b.   Zinc

      c.   Iron

      d.   Aluminum

Answer: A

The density of the marbles was $350g/31cm^3 = 11.3$ cm^3 (SIN)

17   If you are creating a raft that is 175 grams and you want it to float, what must the volume to have a density of 0.5 g/cm^3?

      a.   350 cm^3

      b.   87.5 cm^3

      c.   .003 cm^3

      d.   174.5 cm^3

Answer: A

Volume=$175g/0.5g/cm^3 = 350$ cm^3 (SIN)

18   What is the mass of the cylinder if it is made of iron?

      a.   4.1 grams
      b.   249.6 grams
      c.   0.24 grams
      d.   361.6 grams

Answer: B

Mass=32 cm^3 x 7.8 g/ cm^3=249.6 grams (IOD)

19   If you are filling a toy boat that has a mass of 25 grams and a volume of 600 cm^3 with marbles that each have a mass of 4 grams, how many marbles can you add to the boat before it sinks?

      a.   150
      b.   144
      c.   143
      d.   149

Answer: C

Density has to be less than one for the boat to float. The total mass must be below 600 grams. Boat 25 grams plus 143 marbles at 4 grams each will produce a mass of 597 grams. (EMI)

Reading passage and data for questions 20-25:

The Earth formed approximately 4.6 billion years ago. Initially, the atmosphere consisted of hydrogen, water vapor, methane and carbon oxides. The water vapor condensed 4 billion years ago to form oceans. About 1 billion years ago, blue-green algae in the ocean used the energy from the sun and carbon dioxide to undergo photosynthesis and released oxygen into the atmosphere. Some of this oxygen was split by UV radiation to form single oxygen atoms. These atoms combined with O_2 to form ozone. The ozone layer absorbs harmful UV rays and protects life on Earth from irradiation. The ozone layer was formed approximately 600 million years ago. Prior to this, life on Earth only existed in the ocean and the oxygen level in the atmosphere was 10%. The formation of the ozone layer enabled organisms to live on land.

Millions of Years Ago	Period
0-1.8	Quaternary
1.8-23	Neogene
23-66	Paleogene

66-145	Cretaceous
145-201	Jurassic
201-252	Triassic
252-299	Permian
Life on Earth	Period
1st Humans	Quaternary
Age of Mammals	Neogene
	Paleogene
1st Flowering Plants	Cretaceous
1st Birds	Jurassic
1st Mammals	Triassic
Abundant Reptiles	Permian

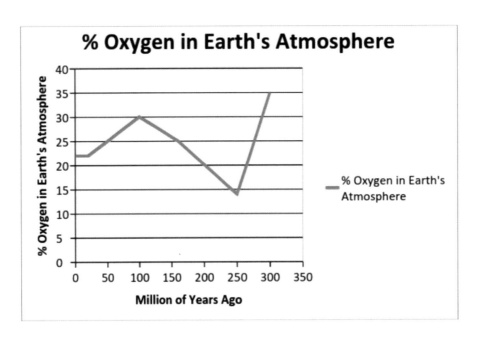

20   Which period had the highest levels of oxygen in the atmosphere?

    a.   Quaternary

    b.   Cretaceous

    c.   Triassic

d. Permian

Answer: D

The highest levels of oxygen occurred 300 MYA during the Permian period. (IOD)

21 During which period did the first warm-blooded animal appear?

   a. Triassic
   b. Quaternary
   c. Jurassic
   d. Permian

Answer: A

Mammals are warm-blooded and they first appeared in the Triassic period. (IOD)

22 How many millions of years ago did the first flowering plant appear?

   a. 145-201
   b. 23-66
   c. 201-252
   d. 66-145

Answer: D

Flowering plants appeared in the Cretaceous period 66-145 MYA. (IOD)

23 Make an inference using Table 1 and Table 2. How many millions of years ago did dinosaurs appear on Earth?

   a. 66-145
   b. 201-252
   c. 252-299
   d. 145-201

Answer: C

Dinosaurs are reptiles. Reptiles were abundant in the Permian period 252-299 MYA. (IOD)

24 What organism lived 650 million years ago?

   a. Flowering plants
   b. Blue-green algae
   c. Insects
   d. Reptiles

Answer: B

Prior to 600 million years ago, all organisms lived in the ocean. (SIN)

25   What was the percent of oxygen in the atmosphere when the first human appeared on Earth?

      a. 35

      b. 20

      c. 24

      d. 22

Answer: D

Human appeared on Earth 1-1.8 MYA. The oxygen level was 22%. (IOD)

Reading passage and data for questions 26-33:

Apple scab is caused by the fungus, *Venturia inaequalis*. It produces dark brown lesions on the leaves, buds, and fruit of apple trees. Apple scab is a problem for apple farmers because it reduces fruit quality and yield. In the spring, the increase in moisture and temperatures causes the spores from the fungus to rise in the air and land on the tree surface. Secondary infections can also occur in the summer. In the winter, the fungus reproduces in the leaf litter creating a new generation of spores. Scientists are trying to determine the lowest dose of fungicide that can be used to reduce the reproduction rate of the fungus and the optimal temperature for the fungus reproduction. Over a 7 day period, at room temperature of 21°C, the fungus spreads 6 cm.

The scientists mixed various amounts of fungicide with agar and plated the fungus spores in petri dishes. They measured how far the fungus spread after 7 days.

Amount of Fungicide (mL)	Amount Fungus Spread (cm)
0.5 mL	6
1.0mL	5
1.5mL	3
2.0mL	3

The scientists performed a second experiment placing the petri dishes with fungus, without fungicide, in various temperatures for 7 days.

Temperature °C	Amount Fungus Spread (cm)
10	9 cm
15	10 cm
20	12 cm
25	12 cm

26   What is the minimum amount of fungicide that can be used to reduce the reproductive rate of the fungus by half?
       a.   0.5 mL
       b.   1.0 mL
       c.   1.5 mL
       d.   2.0 mL
Answer: C
Adding 1.5 mL reduced the spread of the fungus in the petri dish. 2.0 mL reduced the reproduction by the same amount, so 1.5 mL is the least amount that should be used. (IOD)

27   What is the minimal optimal temperature for *Venturia inaequalis* reproduction?
       a.   10°C
       b.   15°C
       c.   20°C
       d.   25°C
Answer: C
The fungus spread 12 cm at 20°C and 25 °C. The minimum temperature is 20°C. (IOD)

28   What is a possible hypothesis for experiment #2?
       a.   When *Venturia inaequalis* is plated in a petri dish with agar and fungicide, the highest level of fungicide will reduce the rate of reproduction.
       b.   When *Venturia inaequalis* is plated in a petri dish with agar, the lowest level of

fungicide at the highest temperature will increase the rate of reproduction.

   c. When *Venturia inaequalis* is plated in a petri dish with agar and fungicide, the highest level of fungicide at the highest temperature will increase the rate of reproduction.

   d. When *Venturia inaequalis* is plated in a petri dish with agar, the optimal temperature for the rate of reproduction is room temperature.

Answer: D

The scientist is determining the optimal temperature for reproduction of *Venturia inaequalis* in petri dishes with agar without fungicide. (EMI)

29   A 20 mL solution of agar + fungicide was used to fill each petri dish in the first experiment. What percent of the solution must be made up of minimum amount of fungicide necessary to reduce the spread of the fungus by half?

   a. 7%

   b. 10%

   c. 12%

   d. 3%

Answer: A

1.5mL is 7% of 20mL. (SIN)

30   The scientists are going to run a third experiment determining the optimal conditions to reduce the reproduction rate of *Venturia inaequalis* by half based on the first and second experiment, which of the following experiment should they run?

   a. An experiment growing *Venturia inaequalis* in petri dishes of agar containing 1.5mL of fungicide at various temperatures.

   b. An experiment growing *Venturia inaequalis* in petri dishes of agar containing various amounts of fungicide at various temperatures.

   c. An experiment growing *Venturia inaequalis* in petri dishes of agar containing various amounts of fungicide at 15°C.

   d. An experiment growing *Venturia inaequalis* in petri dishes of agar containing 2.0mL of fungicide at various temperatures.

Answer: A

1.5mL of fungicide is the minimal amount of fungicide that can be used to reduce the reproduction rate by half. The effectiveness of this amount of fungicide should be tested at various temperatures. (EMI)

31   What is the control in both experiments?

   a. The amount of fungicide used.

   b. The agar in the petri dish.

   c. The reproductive rate of the fungus without fungicide over 7 days.

   d. The reproductive rate of fungus at room temperature over 7 days.

Answer: D

Before the experiments were performed, the scientists determined the growth rate of the fungus for a set period of time and the same temperature. (SIN)

32   The scientists would like to find out if the amount of light impacts the reproduction rate of *Venturia inaequalis*. Using the control from the first two experiments, describe a possible experiment that the scientist could perform.
      Constructed Response(SIN)
      Scoring Guide

Score	Description
2	**The fungus needs to be plated on agar without fungicide for 7 days at room temperature and placed in the dark, low light, and full light.**
1	**The fungus needs to be placed in the dark, low light and full light.**
0	The response does not include placing the fungus in different lighting condition.

33   Predict the amount of fungal spread if 2.5mL of fungicide are used.
      a.   8 cm
      b.   6 cm
      c.   5 cm
      d.   3 cm

Answer: D

Fungal spread at 1.5 and 2.0mL of fungicide added is limited to 3cm, so the spread should be approximately the same if 2.5mL of fungicide are used. (SIN)

Reading passage and data for questions 34-40:

Tennis balls used for tournament play must meet specific guidelines regarding size, weight, bounce and stiffness. A sporting goods company wants to design a faster tennis ball that will meet all of the requirements to be used for tournament play. Tennis balls are currently constructed of rubber with a hollow core, adhesive, and a nap. The nap consists of a mix of wool and artificial fibers. In the first experiment, scientists performed multiple trials and averages were determined using tennis balls with various nap consistency. The tennis balls were launched from a tennis ball machine with the same amount of force in ideal tennis conditions (18°C, 50% humidity and 5mph winds).

The speed of the ball was measured in mph.

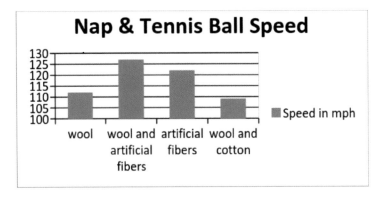

In the second experiment, scientists tested how humidity impacts the speed of tennis balls with nap made of the four different materials. They performed several trials on each nap at the four different humidity levels and determined the average in mph.

Table #1

Nap Material	20% Humidity	40% Humidity	60% Humidity	80% Humidity
Wool	125	112	108	102
Wool & Artificial Fibers	125	126	121	118
Artificial Fibers	120	122	121	122
Wool & Cotton	108	108	102	90

34   Based on the data, what type of nap produces the tennis ball that moves at the highest speed at 50% humidity?

    a.   Wool

    b.   Wool and artificial fibers

    c.   Artificial fibers

    d.   Wool and cotton

Answer: B

The wool and artificial fiber nap covered ball travels at the highest speed. (IOD)

35   List four control variables in this experiment.
      Constructed Response (SIN)
      Scoring Guide

Score	Description
2	**50% humidity, 18°C, tennis ball machine used, and 5 mph winds.**
1	**Humidity, temperature, ball machine, and wind speed.**
0	The response does not include all four of the control variables in the solution.

36   Which nap is not impacted by humidity?
      a. Wool
      b. Wool & Artificial
      c. Artificial Fibers
      d. Wool Cotton
      Answer: C
      According to the data table, the tennis ball with nap made of artificial fiber varied the least at different humidity levels.

37   Which change in humidity resulted in the greatest decrease in speed for the wool & cotton nap?
      a. 20-40%
      b. 40-60%
      c. 60-80%
      d. The change is the same for all humidities.
      Answer: C
      The greatest change in humidity happens between 60 and 80% for the wool & cotton nap, as the speed drops from 102 to 90 mph.

38   What type of nap material should not be used in tournaments that occur in humid conditions?
      a. Wool
      b. Wool & Artificial Fibers
      c. Artificial Fibers
      d. Wool and Cotton
      Answer: D
      Wool and cotton nap tennis balls travel at the lowest speeds at higher humidity levels.
      (IOD)

39   The sporting goods company wants to create and sell tennis balls marketing them as the fastest tennis balls available based on the results of these two experiments. Based on the data, would this be an accurate statement?

    a. The statement is accurate because the scientists performed multiple trials and determined averages for each.

    b. The statement is not accurate because the scientists did not test the tennis ball nap materials at different temperatures and wind speeds.

    c. The statement is accurate because the scientists used controlled variables in the experiment.

    d. The statement is not accurate because the scientists did not use actual tennis players in the experiment.

Answer: B

To be marketed as the fastest tennis ball, **the tennis balls with different nap materials need to be tested at the various weather conditions (wind, temperature)** in which tennis is played. (EMI)

40   Why did the scientists use a ball machine instead of tennis players to perform the experiment?

Answer: The ball machine releases the ball with the same amount of force each time. Even an individual tennis player would hit the ball with variable force.

Constructed Response (SIN)

Scoring Guide

Score	Description
2	**The ball machine consistently releases the ball with the same amount of force each time. An individual tennis player would hit the ball with variable force each time. This would alter the results.**
1	**The ball machine will release the ball with the same force each time.**
0	The response does not include the fact that the ball needs to be released with the same amount of force each time.

Made in the USA
Middletown, DE
04 September 2020

There's no place like home, Itty and Bitty agree.
But the world is vast. There's so much to see.

Cars roll down the driveway, raise dust in the gravel.
Planes fly overhead. Where do they travel?
Our curious minis decide they must roam
And venture beyond the white fences of home.